storytime topics

**Katie Kitching and
Chris Wansborough**

Illustrated by Martin Wansborough

First Published in 1996 by
BELAIR PUBLICATIONS LIMITED
P.O. Box 12, Twickenham, England, TW1 2QL

© 1996 Katie Kitching and Chris Wansborough
Series Editor Robyn Gordon
Designed by Lynn Hooker
Photography by Kelvin Freeman
Typesetting by Belair
Printed and Bound in Singapore through Craft Print Ltd
ISBN 0 947882 78 5

Acknowledgements

The Authors and Publishers would like to thank the children at Buckland Infants School, Chessington, Kingston upon Thames, for their contributions of written work and artwork, during the preparation of this book.

They would also like to thank Bethan Currenti for her generous help in organising artwork; and Amy Blades, Katie Riches, Megan Denton, Charlotte Gibson and Callum Young for their pictures of the Town Mouse and Country Mouse shown on the front cover.

They would like to give special thanks to the Headteacher, Mrs. Baldev Chana, now retired, whose support and encouragement have been invaluable during the preparation of this book, and several previous books in this series.

See Anansi story, page 61

2

Contents

Book References

The above stories are available in many varied editions and collections of stories, from different publishing companies. It was decided not to recommend any particular books, as the stories are so well-known and widely available. However, the authors have included a resumé of the story in each case so that each chapter is complete in itself if you are not able to find a version of the story when you wish to cover that particular topic. In the case of the last four stories (from America, Australia, the Caribbean and India) any other traditional story from that country could be substituted, with the relevant changes being made to the cross-curricular work.

Introduction

Traditional tales have always provided an effective springboard for teaching and learning in the home and at school. From an early age children hear stories from their own culture, and as they grow older they come to hear and appreciate stories from other cultures too. These stories provide effective ways of presenting children with moral issues in terms which they can understand.

In each of the stories used in this book, the underlying moral theme is outlined. Four examples are given for each year group: for children of 4-5 years, 5-6 years, and 6-7 years, but each could be adapted for a different age group.

The stories have been chosen to reflect children's development and growing awareness of wider moral issues. They have also been selected to increase children's knowledge of the world and its diverse cultures.

Traditional nursery tales	➡	More complex traditional tales	➡	Traditional tales from other cultures

The suggested activities cover all subjects in the early years curriculum, and include cross-curricular themes and ideas for assemblies. A resumé is given of the story at the beginning of each section.

Differentiation

It is necessary to differentiate all activities to match the needs, skills and abilities of the individual children. This builds confidence and self-esteem and develops basic skills and concepts. Differentiation can be planned within the range of activities set or within the outcomes expected. For this, careful observation, assessment and record-keeping are required of the teacher to monitor each child's progress.

The activities in this book offer lots of scope for children of different abilities. In the story 'The Sun and the Wind', for example, the whole class brainstormed ideas and words for a class poem about the wind, and drew up a class poem (see photograph page 35). Some children were be encouraged to write their own poems independently (see photograph page 32). Those children who required some support from the teacher referred to the class poem and the vocabulary in order to write their own poems. Children who had not yet reached this stage drew a picture to accompany the poem and dictated their own poem for the teacher to scribe.

Assessment

When planning for each activity, it is helpful if teachers include opportunities for assessment. These may take the form of discussing the activity with the child, of listening in to children's conversations, and of evaluating pieces of work, including writing, drawing, models, constructions, etc. It is useful to keep a selection of what the child has experienced and achieved as a record.

Organisation
Early Stages (4-5 year olds)

Traditional nursery tales present personal and social issues in a meaningful way to young children. They can relate these directly to their own experience, for example 'How can we help the little red hen? How can we help each other?' They provide learning opportunities across the curriculum in real and tangible ways.

These tales can also provide a rich stimulus for role-play, for discussion, and for expressing ideas creatively. Children are thus encouraged to interact with one another purposefully, and to begin to share ideas and play co-operatively together.

Within the classroom, a range of activities can be provided, from those requiring direct teacher input, parent or teacher assistant support, to self-sustaining independent activities. For example, five groups could be working simultaneously, as follows:

THE THREE PIGS

| 1. Test the strengths of bricks, straw and sticks in constructing houses

Teacher focus | 2. Sequence the story in picture form.

Initiated by teacher, then independently | 3. Role-play of the story

Independent | 4. Listen to the story on the tape recorder, OR write the story on a concept keyboard (see photograph)

Independent | 5. Use a programmable toy (for example, Roamer - see text page 14 and photograph page 8)

Parent helper or classroom assistant |

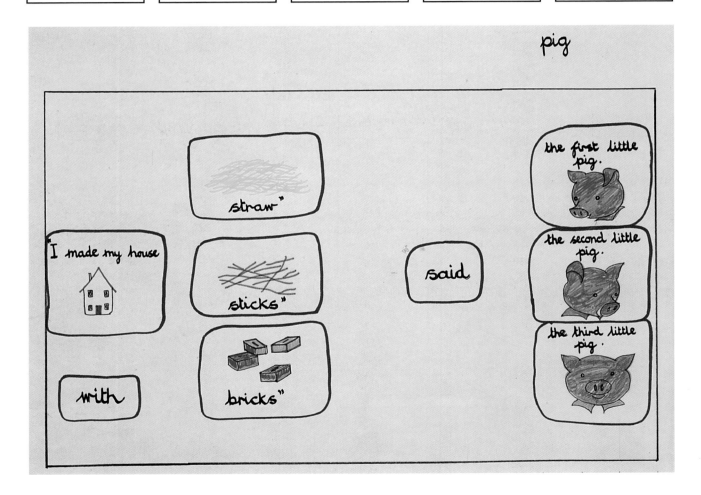

The children are encouraged to develop independence, and as the year progresses the teacher can use this independence to provide activities which are more demanding. Central to this is efficient classroom routines and organisation, accessible resources and careful planning.

Middle Stages
(5-6 year olds)

Traditional tales for this age group should present the children with moral issues which are more complex, but still relevant to their own experience and easily understood. For example 'The Town Mouse and the Country Mouse' highlights that there are differences between people which should be respected and valued. The stories need to be selected to provide opportunities for developing skills in oracy, literacy and numeracy, and for encouraging investigative, expressive and creative abilities.

Strands and ideas within each story can be developed to lead into other areas of enquiry, for example:

THE UGLY DUCKLING (CHANGE)

EGGS	SEASONS	OURSELVES
What is in an egg? How can we cook an egg?	What happens at different times of the year?	How do we change as we grow? (See photograph on page 44)

Activities can be planned on the basis of a whole class approach, group work, paired or individual activities, with a view to encouraging independence in children, extending their learning, and building confidence and motivation.

Further stages (6-7 year olds)

At this age, many children are becoming aware of the world beyond their own experience. Traditional tales such as 'The Wizard Punchkin' (a story from India) are a way of acquainting the children with ideas from other cultures.

Through this, children can begin to appreciate how cultural identity is perpetuated through such means as story-telling.

Many children at this age are developing a growing understanding of wider moral issues which affect the individual and the group in a particular situation.

For example:

THE TALE OF TIDDALIK THE FROG

The effects of a drought	Selfishness of Tiddalik in drinking all the water	Co-operation of all the animals in finding a solution

Strands and ideas from traditional stories can enrich the wider curriculum, particularly in the areas of history and geography and environmental education. They can also act as a stimulus for children to develop investigative strategies using reference materials and to explore areas which are of interest to them. This encourages growing independence in learning, and the ability to collaborate on projects - presenting ideas and information to one another.

See text page 6 (point 5).

THE THREE LITTLE PIGS

Resumé of Story

Three little pigs build their own homes. The first uses straw, the second uses sticks, and the third uses bricks. Along comes a wolf. He blows down the houses of straw and sticks, but cannot blow down the house of bricks. He attempts to catch the pig by climbing down the chimney, but the pig is ready with a pot of hot water.

Telling the Story

Tell the story, rather than read it. Have three bags - one containing straw, one sticks, and one bricks. Seat the children in a circle to tell the story, using the props as they occur in the story, placing them in the centre of the circle. Encourage the children to join in the parts that are repeated - 'I'll huff and I'll puff.....', etc.

Theme of Story (PSE/RE issues)

- Taking care of oneself. What do we mean by 'taking care'? Talk about personal safely. Encourage children to give ideas about keeping safe.
- Nursery stories introduce the idea of good being triumphant and this is an excellent way of introducing the idea of choosing positive options for the good of all. For example, if we are all quiet, the classroom will be a better place for learning.
- Making the right decision. Children need to develop the skill to make appropriate decisions. Talk about situations which could happen in school, and encourage the children to decide how individuals should react. Often this is best expressed in a story. For example, 'Paul made a tower of bricks. He worked carefully and just as he put the last brick on the top Michael walked by and kicked it over. What should Paul do? What should Michael do?'

Assembly Ideas

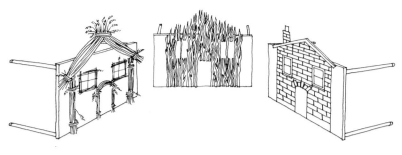

- **Improvise three houses** - tables turned on their sides provide a good frame.
- Re-tell the story using children to play the characters. The first pig could run to the second pig for safety, and so on.
- Say a prayer about keeping safe, and taking care of others.

ENGLISH
Speaking and Listening
- Read different versions of the story, and make a book display.
- Compare the different versions. This story is particularly suitable for predicting. For example: Will the little pigs survive, or does the wolf eat them?
- Re-tell the story from the point of view of one particular pig, or the wolf.
- Did the three pigs choose wisely when they built their houses?
- Was there anything they could have done to keep themselves safe?
- Was the wolf good or bad? What could he have eaten instead of the pigs?

Role Play opportunities
- Make headbands with ears for the pigs and the wolf. If space is available, encourage children to use big building blocks to build houses for the pigs, or use large cardboard cartons.

Further Discussion Points
- Talk about the children's own houses/homes.
- Collect and look at pictures and photographs of different kinds of houses.
- Talk about addresses.
- Name parts of a house - door, window, roof, chimney.
- Who builds houses? Talk about the work of bricklayers, carpenters, etc.

Reading and Writing
- Read different versions of the story of the Three Little Pigs. Make a display.
- **Make zig-zag books** - either individually or as a group.

- **Devise games for word recognition** using vocabulary from the story. A good way of helping children take turns is to pass a model of a pig round the group. The child who has the pig takes a turn.

- Make a word bank of vocabulary from the story.
- Use the story to stimulate emergent writing - introduce speech bubbles.
- Collect pig poems in a pig-shaped book.
- Make a collection of information books about pigs and houses.
- **Write out a favourite poem** for children to illustrate.

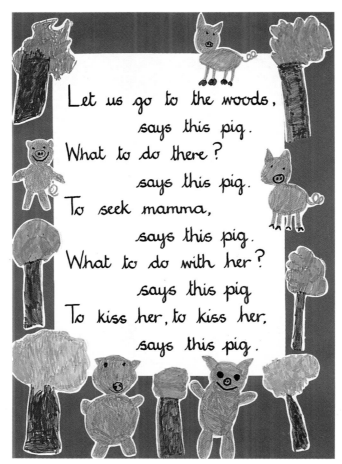

Let us go to the woods,
  says this pig.
What to do there?
  says this pig.
To seek mamma,
  says this pig.
What to do with her?
  says this pig
To kiss her, to kiss her,
  says this pig.

MATHEMATICS

- Sequence the houses (see the border of picture on page 9).
- **Use the pigs and houses in number stories.**
  For example, three houses - how many windows?
  Three pigs - how many ears?

How many doors ? ☐   How many ears ? ☐

How many windows ? ☐   How many legs ? ☐

How many chimneys ? ☐   How many tails ? ☐

- Use houses to investigate 2-dimensional shapes. Use triangle for roof, square for house, oblong for door, and so on. Record this by using gummed paper, or draw round 2-dimensional shapes positioned to make a house.
- Use 3-dimensional shapes (bricks and blocks) to build houses. Which shapes are the best for building houses? How many bricks have you used?
- **Devise worksheets using 2-dimensional shapes.**

Join the word and the shape

triangle

oblong

square

circle

how many triangles ? ☐

how many oblongs ? ☐

how many squares ? ☐

how many circles ? ☐

- **Make a board game** (see photograph).
- Make a survey of the numbers of children's own homes. (See Art and Craft for extension of this idea.)

SCIENCE
- Examine and describe straw, sticks and bricks.
- How did the wolf knock down the houses? How else could he have done this? Why did the brick house stay standing?
- Talk about safety on building sites, and the need for helmets, etc.

HUMANITIES - History and Geography
- Sequence the story (see photograph of zig-zag book, page 10).
- Go for a walk round school inside and outside. Look for different kinds of brickwork.
- If possible, take a walk round the immediate locality of the school. Look at the houses there. During and after taking a walk, describe directions you took and what you could see.

DESIGN AND TECHNOLOGY
- Ask the children how they would build houses of the materials the pigs used. What would hold them together?
- Follow this by building houses of straw, sticks and bricks on a large board. Test the strength of the structures - a hairdryer could be used.
- Use found materials to make three houses for I.T. and Humanities activities. (See photograph on page 8.)

- **Make pig puppets** using cardboard plates joined with butterfly clips (see photograph).

ART AND CRAFT
- Make a large wall display of the story using mixed media, with a border of the three houses (see photograph on page 9).
- Draw the three little pigs and their houses.
- Draw the wolf. What would make him look fierce? What would make him look gentle?
- **Make picture cards of houses.** Put your own number on the front door.

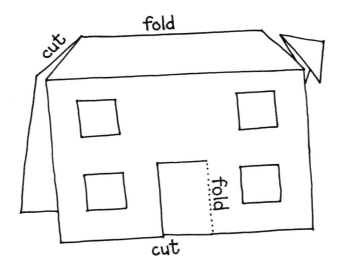

P.E., DRAMA, MOVEMENT
- Dramatise building a house, using body movements to indicate sawing, hammering, etc.
- Re-tell the story in mime, building up each section and finishing with the whole story.
- The wolf needs to keep fit, ready to blow down the houses. Think of ways he could do this!
- Use apparatus in P.E. to indicate the location of the three houses. Children follow the route the wolf took.

MUSIC
- **Tell the story using instruments.** Select an instrument for each of the characters using contrasting sounds. Think of 'house building' sounds and a sound for the houses falling.
- Make a set of rhythms based on the story, for clapping or playing percussion instruments.

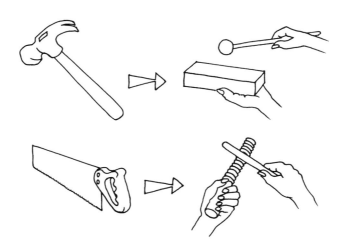

INFORMATION TECHNOLOGY
- Make a concept keyboard overlay of story (see photograph on page 6).
- Use Roamer (or similar toy which can be programmed), disguised as the wolf. Can children make the 'wolf' visit each of the pigs' houses?

GOLDILOCKS AND THE THREE BEARS

Resumé of Story

The Three Bears live in the woods in a little cottage. One morning they make porridge, but it is too hot to eat, so they go out for a walk while it cools. Meanwhile, Goldilocks is lost in the woods. She finds the cottage, goes in and tries the porridge. She eats Baby Bear's porridge, then tries the chairs and breaks Baby Bear's chair. Finally, she tries the beds, falling asleep in Baby Bear's bed. The bears return, discover Goldilocks and chase her away.

Telling the Story

Collect the following big, middle-sized and small items: saucepans, spoons, bowls, cups and saucers, plates, etc. Use these when telling the story to emphasise the concept of big, middle-sized and small. Use voice intonation to depict the different characters. Encourage children to join in the parts that are repeated.

Theme of Story (PSE/RE issues)

- Personal safety. Develop the theme further by discussing how children can take care of themselves. Where are they safe? Should they wander off on their own? What should they do if they get lost? Who should they ask for help?
- Respecting the property of others. Ask the children to think about their favourite toy. How would they feel if someone took or broke their toy? Extend this idea to classroom or communal possessions. If a toy is broken or mislaid, will others be able to play with it?
- Saying sorry. Situations frequently arise in the classroom, accidental or deliberate, when children need to say 'sorry'. It is important to develop an attitude of genuine remorse, and this frequently involves discussions with the individuals and/or with the class. Try to establish how the wronged party feels, and explain that when saying sorry we must really mean it. Occasionally teachers need to say sorry to children - a responsibility not to be avoided!

Assembly Ideas
• Re-tell the story, with children miming the characters.

• **Show children's paintings of why Goldilocks was wrong** (see photograph). Children explain why they think Goldilocks was wrong. This could be developed into a question and answer dialogue to which children contribute ideas about respect for property and keeping safe.

ENGLISH
Speaking and Listening
• Collect and tell different versions of the story.
• Compare the different versions. How are they similar? How are they different?
• Discuss and predict how the story could develop.
• Re-tell the story in episodes.
• What did the bears have to do after Goldilocks had gone?
• Was Goldilocks wise to go into a strange house? Do we go into other people's houses? Was she wrong to use other people's belongings? Should she have eaten the porridge, broken the chair, and slept in the little bed? Did she think how Little Bear might feel? Should she have said 'sorry'?

Role Play opportunities
Set up the play area as the interior of the Three Bears' cottage. **Provide headbands** with big ears, middle-sized ears and little ears, and one with wool plaits. Have big, middle-sized and small cutlery and crockery so that children can set the table; also chairs, cushions, saucepans, etc., to encourage sequencing and matching.

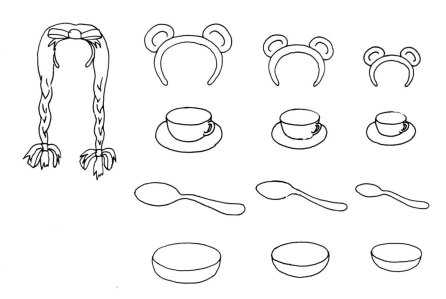

Further Discussion Points
- Make a collection of children's own teddy bears.
- Encourage children to talk about their own bear. Who gave it to you? Where do you keep it? What is its name?
- Play circle games using bears:
- Put three bears in the centre of the circle and talk about their size, colour, shape, texture, etc. Ask children to close their eyes. Cover one bear with a cloth and ask children to describe the bear which is covered.
- Children sit in a circle holding their own bears. They take turns round the circle to say a sentence about their bear. For example, 'My bear is little and I call him Smartie', 'My bear has a red bow', etc.
- Devise other circle games.
- Make porridge. Go for a walk while it cools. (Perhaps arrange with another staff member to act as Goldilocks in your absence!)

Reading and Writing
- Read books about Goldilocks and the Three Bears, and other stories which centre on bears.
- Make a class book about Goldilocks and the Three Bears, either with teacher acting as scribe or using the computer to print the text - children illustrate.
- Use children's own ideas to write captions for paintings, wall displays, etc.
- Make a word bank of words which children may need when they write about the three bears (see photograph on page 7).
- With teacher as scribe, write a class poem about a particular bear.
- Use part of the story to stimulate emergent writing. For example, write about what Baby Bear said to Goldilocks.

MATHEMATICS
- Make place settings for the three bears, encouraging one-to-one correspondence.
- Sequence bears using colour and size.
- **Devise problem-solving activities** using bears.

Measure the bears' cottage with cubes

The cottage is ☐ cubes wide
The cottage is ☐ cubes high

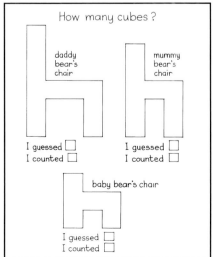

How many cubes?

daddy bear's chair

mummy bear's chair

I guessed ☐
I counted ☐

I guessed ☐
I counted ☐

baby bear's chair

I guessed ☐
I counted ☐

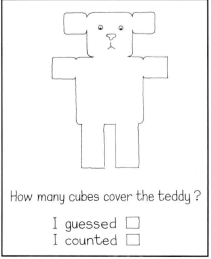

How many cubes cover the teddy?

I guessed ☐
I counted ☐

We made covers for the bears' beds.

We needed 9 squares for mummy.

We needed 16 squares for daddy.

We needed 4 squares for baby.

- **Bedspreads - sew with binca** (see photograph).
- Develop comparative language using bears - big, middle-sized, little, etc.
- Use teddy bear collection for weighing and measuring activities.
- Make a number line using bear shapes.

colour the bears

- **Devise activities to introduce data handling** (see line drawings).
- Make a cottage (see Design and Technology) for the bears, and use this to illustrate opposites and positions - up, down, in, out, in front, behind, etc.

SCIENCE
- Use oats in cookery - make porridge, oatcakes, oat bread, etc.
- Examine different kinds of oats - rolled oats, oat grains, oatmeal, etc. What happens to rolled oats when we make porridge?

- What sort of body covering do bears have? Why do you think they are covered with fur? Use fur-covered hot water bottles to demonstrate how fur keeps things warm. How do we keep warm? Describe sensations of warmth and cold.
- Make porridge. While it cools go for a walk round school or the school grounds, looking at the environment.

HUMANITIES - History and Geography
- Sequence the story.
- Could the story really have happened? Talk about *real* and *make-believe.*
- Talk about *old* and *new* - **use teddy bear collection to make a time-line** (see photograph).

- Make a map of the woods and suggest a route for Goldilocks and the Three Bears so they do not meet!
- Where do real bears come from? Find information books about different species, and locate these on a world map.
- Go for a walk while porridge cools (See Speaking and Listening). Discuss route taken with the children.

DESIGN AND TECHNOLOGY
- Make teddy bears using butterfly clips to joint arms, legs and body. Draw your bear.
- Use construction toys to make a cart to carry a teddy bear.
- How could we mend Little Bear's chair?
- **Make a cottage for the Three Bears** using large cardboard boxes. Furnish it with appropriate sized furniture, and use it to illustrate prepositions (see Maths).
- Think of others ways we could carry a bear. Make a model, using found materials.
- Sew binca squares for bedspreads. Design bedspreads for the bears' beds (see photograph page 18).

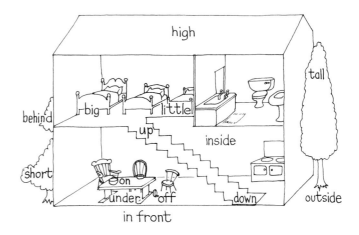

ART AND CRAFT

Can you match a bear with a picture?

We drew our teddy-bears.

- **Children make life portraits of their own teddy bears** (see photograph above).
- Use mixed media to make a group picture of the Three Bears and their different sized possessions (see photograph on page 15).
- Paint pictures of bears.
- Use bear motifs to make sequence borders for wall pictures.
- Illustrate class books of Goldilocks and the Three Bears.

P.E., DRAMA, MOVEMENT
- Devise sequences using the Three Bears. How would they move? Use body movements to show the different bears.
- Act out the story in mime, developing each part of the story and finally acting out the whole story.
- Set up a role play area (see Speaking and Listening).

MUSIC
- Use instruments to depict the different characters in the story and link with drama and movement.
- Learn the song 'When Goldilocks went to the house of the bears' (*Okki-Tokki-Unga*, A&C Black).
- **Make up rhythms to clap using phrases from the story** - for example:

here is broken chair Goldilocks

hot porridge

go home bad girl

big daddy bear

INFORMATION TECHNOLOGY
- Devise concept keyboard overlay.
- Use software with teddy bear theme.

THE LITTLE RED HEN

(Planting and Growing)

Resumé of Story

The Little Red Hen finds some grains of wheat. She asks her friends to help her plant, water, cut, thresh and mill the grain, but they are all too lazy. When she has baked the bread they all want a share, but since they had not helped her, she eats it herself.

Telling the Story

Sit children in a circle, and put a cloth in the centre.

Use artefacts to demonstrate each stage of the story: small spade, watering can, hoe, sickle, small cart and sack for carrying, stones for grinding, dish of flour, loaf of bread. Place the artefacts on the cloth as the story unfolds. Encourage discussion about the artefacts when the story has been told.

Theme of Story (PSE/RE issues)

- Working and doing our best. Explore, with the children, what it means to do our best. Use examples of children's work to illustrate the idea of 'best'. Discuss with individual children what they like about their own work. Do this sensitively with regard to the child's stage of development.
- Helping each other. Discuss ways in which children can help each other, how they can help adults, etc. Make a list of things they can do to help: for example, tidying up, washing paint pots, sweeping up sand, etc. Extend this idea into caring for our environment.
- Sharing. Talk about sharing and giving. Young children are still learning to share toys and games, and often need help to develop the social skills involved. Use classroom situations to illustrate and develop the concept of sharing and caring. Cookery is an excellent vehicle for this: a group cooks and shares the product with the rest of the class. The children who cook gain self-esteem and a sense of responsibility. The rest of the class enjoy the food and learn to say 'thank you', developing social skills.

Assembly Ideas

- Resources: Masks or head-dresses, models of how we can help the Red Hen (see Design and Technology section), loaves of bread, musical instruments.
- Tell the story of the Little Red Hen, using children in head-dresses or masks to depict the characters.

- Use 'Who will help me?' rhythms (see Music) for each of the different stages of the story.
- Re-tell the story, but this time a child with a model of an implement (see Design and Technology) interrupts at the appropriate moment, saying that he or she will help. End by giving a loaf of bread to each class in the school. How can we help each other in school?

ENGLISH
Speaking and Listening
- Collect different versions and compare.
- Which animals appear in each version?
- Predict the ending. Will the hen share the bread or eat it herself?
- Sequence the story with a child telling each section (see photograph on page 5).
- How could we help the Little Red Hen?

Role Play opportunities
Make salt dough biscuits and papier mâché cakes and loaves of bread. Use these to create a baker's shop, giving opportunities for buying and selling activities. Begin with free play, then introduce 'One penny for one item' shopping.

Further Discussion Points
- Talk about farms and farmers.
- Find other stories which have a red hen as a character (for example, Red Hen and Sly Fox, and Henny Penny).

Reading and Writing
- Make a class book of the story, with teacher as scribe, perhaps using a computer to print the text.
- **Use animal names** - dog, pig, cat, hen, as a starting point to investigate word families.

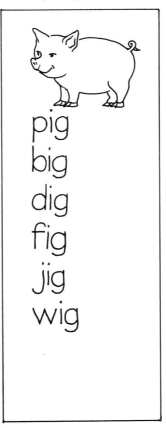

pig
big
dig
fig
jig
wig

cat
bat
fat
hat
mat
pat
rat
sat

- Look at and make a collection of information books about farms.
- Compile a recipe book of different kinds of bread.
- Record planting and growing activities.

MATHEMATICS

- **Use role play area for buying and selling activities** - free play to start with, then one item for 1p, finally introducing 2p, 5p and 10p coins.

- Use the windmill to introduce the idea of turning (see photograph on page 25). What else turns?
- Make and bake salt dough biscuits and cakes, some large, some small. These can be used in balancing activities to demonstrate concepts of heavy and light. Make a set of things which are the same weight.
- Measure the growth of plants such as beans, using non-standard measures, for example, Multilink cubes.
- Use plant growth to encourage language to describe length - long, short, tall, etc., and to compare size.

SCIENCE

- Examine and describe different sorts of grain, including wheat.
- Make bread. Try several different kinds: soda bread, flat breads (naan, chapati), as well as yeast breads. Examine and describe different sorts of flour: wholemeal flour, white flour, cornflour.
- Use the story as a basis for planting and growing activities of all kinds.

- **What do plants need for healthy growth?** Devise simple ways of demonstrating the need for water and light.

• **Look at different seeds.** Examine closely, and discuss what they will grow into (see photograph).

HUMANITIES - Geography and History

• **Discuss what is found on a farm.** Use a toy farmyard to illustrate.

• Provide sheets of paper taped to tabletop with farmyard animals or buildings so that children can make their own farmyard maps.
• Look at pictures of windmills. Describe how they were used years ago to grind grain.
• Think about the work of farmers, millers and bakers.
• Sequence the process of how a loaf of bread is made: the farmer sows seed, grows corn, harvests corn, etc.

DESIGN AND TECHNOLOGY

• How could we grind wheat into flour? Discuss how this was done using millstones. Try using two flat stones to grind wheat grains.
• Think of ways we could help the Little Red Hen. Draw and make implements: spade to dig, ways of scattering seed, etc.
• Make head-dresses or masks for the characters in the story. Use these in assembly.

We made windmills.

- **Make windmills.** This is an excellent activity to introduce Design and Technology tools: clamp, saw, hammer, etc.
- Make salt dough and papier mâché biscuits, cakes and bread for the baker's shop (see Maths).
- Make some bread dough and use it to make a variety of shapes.

ART AND CRAFT
- Make pictures of how we could help the Little Red Hen. The children could draw self-portraits (or use photographs) to attach to their own ideas. (See photograph on page 5.)
- Use collage and felt pens to make windmill pictures. Two children could collaborate to make a picture (see photograph above).

P.E., DRAMA, MOVEMENT
- Tell the story in mime: finding the grains, digging the soil, watering, etc.
- Act out a day in the life of a farmer. Ask the children to suggest activities, for example, feeding hens, milking cows, ploughing field, etc.

MUSIC
- Sing songs about farms and farm animals.
- Make rhythms with the repeated parts of the story ('Who will help me?' 'Not I', said the cat, etc.). Use body percussion as you say the words. Later, use classroom instruments.
- Think of sounds to accompany each stage of the story: for example, maracas for sowing the seed; rain stick or bells for watering; a cymbal hit with a comb for cutting the corn, etc. Re-tell the story with the instruments joining in at the appropriate moment.

INFORMATION TECHNOLOGY
- Use the concept keyboard to tell part of the story.
- Use a word processor to practise word families suggested in Reading and Writing section.

THE GINGERBREAD MAN

Resumé of Story

An old woman bakes a gingerbread man but, once cooked, he runs away. The old woman, the old man, a cow and a horse all chase after him but cannot catch him. He comes to a river, but he cannot swim. A fox offers to carry him across. Once on the other side, the fox eats him.

Telling the Story

Use cut-outs of the characters in the story to emphasise the sequence (see photograph). Encourage children to join in the parts that are repeated - 'Run, run, as fast as you can, you can't catch me, I'm the gingerbread man.'

Theme of Story (PSE/RE issues)

- Discuss with the children what 'boasting' means. Ask them to give their own ideas about boasting and bragging. Develop the theme into listening about what others can do, or what others have got, and not trying to better the achievements or possessions of others. This is a difficult area for young children and it is worth spending time helping them to develop consideration for the achievements and abilities of others. A circle game is a good starting point: children take turns to think of something that their neighbour does well.
- Be careful whom you trust. This concept is very important and should be approached with sensitivity and thought. Children should be made aware of issues of personal safety: of when to say 'no' and whom they can trust. Make a list of people who will help: teachers, policeman or policewoman, etc. Explain, in terms the children understand, how to say 'no' and walk away from threatening situations.

Assembly Ideas

- Act out the story using a child for each character.
- A group of children could play the 'Run, run, as fast as you can' rhythms on percussion instruments (see Music) each time it occurs.
- Talk about personal safety and emphasise the need for care when we are out and about.

ENGLISH
Speaking and Listening
• Collect and read different versions of the story.
• Is the main character called the Gingerbread Man or the Gingerbread Boy?
• Are the characters the same in all the versions, or are there more in some?
• What does the Gingerbread Man say to everyone he meets?

Role Play opportunities
• The story introduces the theme of journeys. There are many ways that the role play area could develop this: for example, a train, or an aeroplane, or a travel agency.
• Alternatively, children could freely interpret the story. Give them labels to wear and encourage them to devise a route for the action.

Reading and Writing
• Make individual books about the Gingerbread Man.
• Use a large recipe card (see photograph on page 29) when making gingerbread men, showing the children an example of reading for a purpose.
• **Use cut-outs of characters to introduce vocabulary-:** 'I am the old woman', 'I am the ......' etc. (see photograph above.

MATHEMATICS
* Arrange a series of gingerbread men by size.

* **Play a gingerbread man/woman matrix game** (see photograph).

* **Measure a gingerbread man shape using cubes.**
  Which door can he go through?

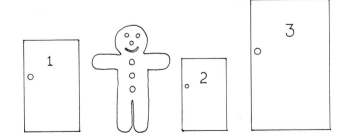

The gingerbread man is ☐ cubes tall.
He can go through door ☐.

* Use the story to develop concepts of position and movement: forwards, backwards, turning, etc. Send a child on a 'Gingerbread Man journey' (two steps forwards, turn, three steps back, etc.). How will the Gingerbread Man get back? Is the return journey the same length as the outward journey?

SCIENCE
* Look at ground ginger and other spices. Do they have different smells? Compare the colours.
* Make playdough gingerbread men. Can the children name the external parts of the body - head, legs, neck, etc.?

28

- **Bake gingerbread men.** Discuss the cookery process. Describe the ingredients and how they change as they are mixed. What is the dough like? Does it change shape when it is kneaded? What happens when the gingerbread men are cooked in the hot oven?

HUMANITIES - History and Geography

- **Describe the Gingerbread Man's journey** - out of the house, down the road, across the field, through the wood, etc.

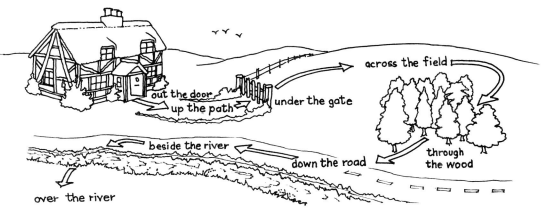

- Think about the things he saw on his way - geographical features, etc.
- Sequence the cookery process. Use pictures which children cut out and put in correct order.

DESIGN AND TECHNOLOGY

- **Make Gingerbread Men glove puppets** (see photograph).
- Use collage techniques (fabric, fur fabric, cotton wool, etc.) to make the characters in the story. Mount these on small boxes so they stand out from board (see photograph on page 26).
- Make an outfit for a gingerbread man. What clothes would he wear in hot, cold, wet weather?

ART AND CRAFT

- Gingerbread people paintings. Paint the basic shape and add printed buttons, mouth, eyes, flowers, grass, sun.
- Paint a series of pictures to tell the story, and use as a big class book or a wall story.

P.E., DRAMA, MOVEMENT

- The story can be told using children to act the characters. Arrange the room so that children can make a circuit. Choose a Gingerbread Man. As the story is told, choose a child for the next character, to follow the Gingerbread Man round the circuit.
- **In P.E., arrange apparatus** to mark the Gingerbread Man's journey. Children follow the route of the story.

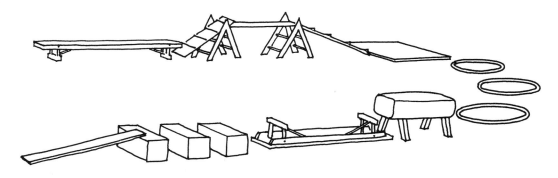

MUSIC

- Use the words of the Gingerbread Man to make clapping rhythms. Use different 'body sounds' for each phrase. For example, Run, run, as fast as you can (clap hands); You can't catch me (slap knees); I'm the Gingerbread Man (tap head). When children have become familiar with the patterns, introduce instruments instead.

INFORMATION TECHNOLOGY

- Use a programmable toy (for example, Roamer) to make a Gingerbread Man journey.
- Record the Gingerbread Man rhythms on a tape recorder.

THE SUN AND THE WIND

(Story source - an Aesop fable , Ancient Greece)

Resumé of Story

The Sun and the Wind cannot agree on who is the stronger, so they put this to the test. Whoever can make the man take his coat off will be the winner. The Wind blows harder and harder but the man only pulls his coat more tightly around him to keep warm. Then it is the Sun's turn. He shines gently down on the man, making him hotter and hotter. Eventually the man takes his coat off, and the Sun is the winner.

Telling the Story

- Divide the children into two groups, one taking the role of the Wind, the other that of the Sun. Discuss with them how they will play their parts. Tell the story, and indicate to each group when they can participate. The children could be sitting or standing.
- Use percussion instruments to represent the Sun and the Wind.
- Encourage the children to predict who will win, and why.

Theme of Story (PSE/RE issues)

- The use of force is not necessarily the best way to achieve a desired outcome.

Assembly Ideas

- The story can be narrated in sections by a group of children with individuals playing the three characters. Simple head-dresses or masks could emphasise the characters of the Wind and the Sun. The actors can mime or speak their parts.
- Use percussion instruments to emphasise the actions of the Wind and the Sun.
- Issues to consider: Use children's own experiences to elaborate on the themes. How do we go about getting others to do things we want? Do we try to force them, or do we persuade them and talk to them about it? How do we want to be treated by others?

ENGLISH
Speaking and Listening

• The sequence of events in this story is straightforward and provides an opportunity for children to recall the story and re-tell it to others - using movement and sound as appropriate.

• Read contrasting weather poems to the children - drawing their attention to conventions such as rhyming, layout, use of capital letters, etc. Encourage children to read and to learn poems. Add actions and sounds, if appropriate. Encourage careful listening skills.

• **Brainstorm words to describe the Wind and the Sun,** and record these. Discuss their meaning.

Reading and Writing

• Use the words to write a class poem with children offering contributions. Encourage them to think about the structure of the poem. Does it need to rhyme? How long should each line be? Which descriptive words should be included? Are made-up words allowed? How are full stops and capital letters to be used? (See photograph on page 35.)

• **Individual poems could be written on a word processor,** and illustrated by the children.

The wind is jumping up and down
To his excitement the wind blows and blows
But can't take the man's coat off
Now it is the sunshine
And the sun burns down and wins.
The end

• Read stories set in different weather conditions. What effect did the weather have on events in these stories? How did the people or animals in the story react?

• What do we do when it rains, snows, is sunny, etc? Write about a rainy/snowy/sunny day as appropriate. Provide a word bank of weather words to support emergent writing.

• **Make a zig-zag book** about different aspects of the weather.

• Make a class book about the weather.
• Investigate and collect words ending in 'y', for example, windy, rainy, sunny, cloudy. Make children aware of this ending. Also of use of 'ing' in words such as raining, snowing, and in commonly used words such as going, doing, coming, etc. Learn some of these spellings.
• Highlight punctuation and its use in poems and stories, and in children's own written work.
• Investigate different sorts of weather conditions and the effect these have on our environment and on us.
• Discuss ways in which we can achieve what we want with the help of others, and the best ways of going about this. How can we help others?

MATHEMATICS
• Make a weather chart by recording the weather each day for a month. Analyse the results with the children (see photograph on page 34).
• How many rainy, sunny, etc., days were there? Draw up a database and record in different ways (for example, bar chart, pie chart - with use of computer), what has been observed.
• Look for circles and other spheres in the environment. Compare these with other 2-dimensional and 3-dimensional shapes. What are their properties and what are they particularly useful for? Make sets of objects of different shapes.
• **Devise 'sun' sums** to give practice with number bonds to ten.

SCIENCE
• What effect does the weather have on plants, animals and people?
• How does the rain, sun, wind, etc., help to provide the conditions for life? Specific examples can help. For example, the wind helps to blow seeds from plants to grow new plants elsewhere.
• **Try growing plants in different conditions**, for example, in the dark without water, to illustrate the requirements for growing.

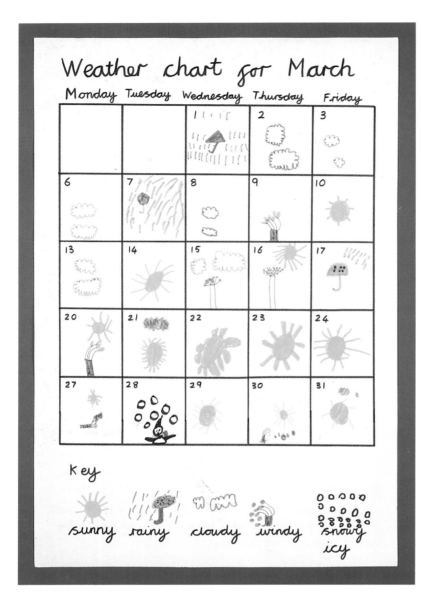

- Investigate materials which are suitable to withstand a particular sort of weather, and which will offer protection: for example, waterproof coats, boots and umbrellas for the rain; cotton shorts and tops, sunhats, sunglasses and suntan lotion in hot sunshine (see Design and Technology).

HUMANITIES - History and Geography

- Note words to describe past, present and future, especially in relation to the weather chart. For example: What was the weather like yesterday? What is it like today? What might it be like tomorrow?
- Look back over the weather chart and recall the weather in the past.
- Find out about how people in the past protected themselves from the weather. For example, parasols and fans were used by ladies in the past to protect themselves against the sun. Layers of clothes made of thick wool and fur were worn in the past to protect people from the cold.
- Investigate how the weather and our climate affects how we live, and what we do.
- Take a specific topic, such as homes, and consider questions like: Why do we have sloping roofs? Why do we have thick walls? Why do we often use bricks and tiles or slates? Compare our homes with homes in other lands with different climates.

DESIGN AND TECHNOLOGY

- Design an outfit suitable for a particular type of weather, either by drawing and labelling it, or by using appropriate materials to make a 2-dimensional design on paper or a 3-dimensional design using a 'model' such as a teddy bear or a doll, depending on skills. Explain why these materials are suitable. Test them if possible. For example: Are materials chosen for wet weather waterproof?
- Make a kite and decorate it. Test to see if it will fly in the wind.

ART AND CRAFT

- Make a class collage using paint, paper and material, to illustrate the story of the Sun and Wind, and two different types of weather (see photograph on page 31).
- Paint and draw individual pictures to illustrate different sorts of weather. Emphasise the importance of details and of colours used.
- Look at famous paintings of different types of weather. How do we know what the weather is like? (For example: Sun - Van Gogh ('The Siesta'); Rain - Renoir ('Les Parapluies'); Snow - Monet ('La Pie').

P.E., DRAMA, MOVEMENT

- Use contrasts of pace in all aspects of P.E. and movement. Reinforce these contrasts in action with correct vocabulary, and encourage children to use this to describe what they are doing.

- Contrast the characters of the Sun and of the Wind through movement, for example, fast, strong, jerky movements for the wind, and slow, smooth, controlled, expansive movements for the sun. Play other weather 'characters', for example the Snow, Jack Frost, the Fog. How would you communicate what they are like?
- Contrast variations in movement according to the weather: for example, splashing in puddles, sliding on ice and stepping through snow.
- Work in pairs to mime leisure activities in different weather, for example, a snowball fight, playing ball on the beach, building a sandcastle.

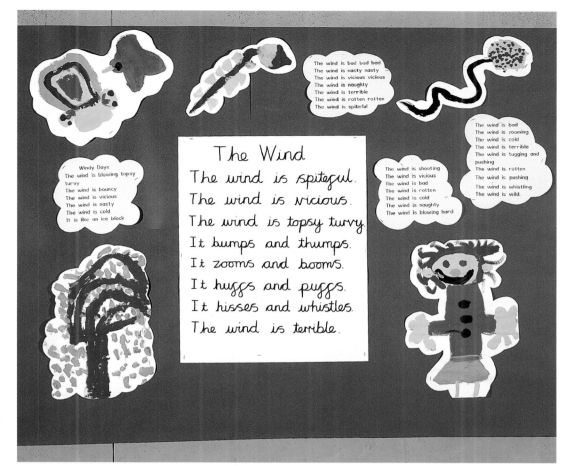

MUSIC

- Investigate the variety of sounds which can be made by percussion instruments. Decide which instruments and sounds best illustrate a particular type of weather, and why.
- Create a musical collage with contrasts of rhythm and timbre, with one group of children playing the sounds for sunshine, another for rain, etc., with the teacher acting as a conductor and bringing each group in at a different time. A suitable progression could be sunshine followed by the onset of rain and a storm, and then sunshine returning as the storm fades away.
- **Investigate crescendo and diminuendo** - getting louder and softer (for example, the storm), responding to signs from the teacher or another child. Record the changes.

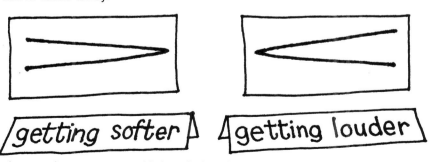

- Learn songs and rhymes about weather, and accompany with hand-clapping, body movements or percussion instruments.
- Listen to famous music that illustrates a particular type of weather, for example, Beethoven's 'Pastoral Symphony'. What can you hear? Which instruments are playing? Provide reference books or charts to link sounds heard with instruments' appearance. Invite musicians into school.

THE THREE BILLY GOATS GRUFF

(Story source - A traditional tale from Western Europe)

Resumé of Story)

The Three Billy Goats Gruff have a problem. They have eaten all their grass and need to get to the fresh long green grass on the other side of the river. There is a bridge across the river, but underneath lives a fierce Troll who is hungry for his supper. What are they to do? Little Billy Goat Gruff is the first to go over the bridge - 'trip, trap, trip, trap'. Up jumps the Troll . 'Who's that crossing over my bridge?' he roars. 'I'm a troll, fol-de-rol, and I'll eat you for my supper'. Little Billy Goat Gruff manages to escape by telling the Troll that he is only small, and his brother, who is bigger and who will make a better meal, is coming next. Soon he is enjoying the grass on the other side of the river.

The same happens with the middle-sized Billy Goat Gruff, and he too tricks the Troll into letting him cross the bridge. Finally, great big Billy Goat Gruff crosses the bridge but when the Troll threatens him, he puts down his head and throws the Troll into the river with his horns. That is the end of the Troll, and the Billy Goats are able to enjoy the new grass.

Telling the Story

• Tell from memory, rather than read the story, emphasising the language which introduces rhyme and alliteration, for example, 'trip-trap'.
• Indicate through pauses, gestures or voice, when the children can join in with the refrain. For example, 'I'm a troll, fol-de-rol', **or use word cards**, for example 'trip-trap' for the children to read.

• Use vocal range to convey the characters' personalities.
• Predict what will happen to each Billy Goat and to the Troll.
• Use clapping rhythms to emphasise actions, such as the Billy Goats crossing the bridge.
• Re-tell the story from the Troll's point of view, with the children's help. How did he feel?
• Read different versions of the story. Compare illustrations and use of English as well as content.

Theme of Story (PSE/RE issues)

• Respecting the needs and rights of others. Look at an issue from different points of view. Who was right? Who was wrong? Consider the importance of 'give and take'.

Assembly Ideas

• Tell or act the story using the teacher and/or individual children, with the rest of the class joining in to emphasise the refrains or repetitive actions. Use simple props such as staging blocks for the bridge.
• Use clapping rhythms or percussion instruments to emphasise the refrains and the personalities of the characters.
• Illustrate the sequence of the story with paintings, etc.

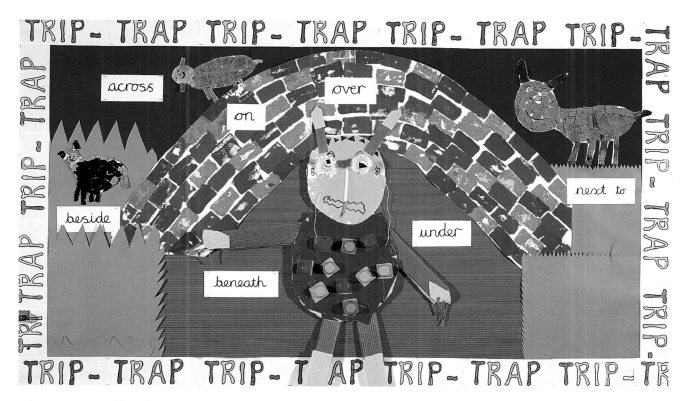

- Issues to consider: Do we need to see things from other people's points of view? Can we work together with others to get what we need through sharing and co-operation? How can we find out and think about each other's needs in school and at home?

ENGLISH
Speaking and Listening
- Children act out the story in sequence in a small group for the rest of the class, using their own words and with support from the teacher as necessary. Props can be improvised.
- **Use masks and labels** to encourage children to take on a particular role.

- Set up a role play area with blocks as a bridge. Re-tell the story from the Troll's point of view, and act this out. What sort of character is the Troll? What words describe him? What is it like for him to live under a bridge? Where else could he go?
- What would have happened if events had taken a different turn, for example, if the Troll had eaten the Little Billy Goat Gruff; if there had been another way across the river; if the Troll had decided to share his bridge?
- Consider the words and the language used in the story in terms of repetition, alliteration, rhythm and rhyme.
- Make up own rhymes and share these.

- Look at prepositions used in the story: for example, over, under, across, beside, in, on, next to, near, through, behind, in front of, etc.
- Tape different versions of the story for the children to listen to on headphones and to follow in the book.

READING AND WRITING
- Retell the story in pictorial and/or written form, depending on ability. Use a zig-zag book to aid sequencing, numbering the sections from 1 to 4, left to right.
- Use a word bank to support emergent writing. Words can be glued on to card and removed easily from a carpet tile or similar material if backed with Velcro (see example on page 7).
- Draw a portrait of the Troll and write about him. Is your Troll fierce or is he sad?
- **Write a rhyme for your Troll and draw a picture to illustrate it.** For example, 'I'm a troll in a hole'. Make a class book to read and share.

A goat in a boat   *A troll in a hole*

- Make a poster with a caption warning the Three Billy Goats Gruff about the Troll.
- Collect different versions of the story. Compare the story itself, the language used and the illustrations. Put different versions on tape for children to listen to. Use parents' voices.
- Collect poems and stories about make-believe characters like the Troll, and make a display.
- Provide non-fiction books about goats and other animals who eat grass.
- **Investigate words beginning with the blends** - *br, tr, gr*. Make sets of these words. Practise handwriting and spelling using worksheets and games based on these sounds.

Make a bridge of words beginning with **tr**

- Learn to spell some prepositions, for example, over, under, up, down, etc., and use in writing. Make a word bank to support.
- Collect and read poems and stories about rivers.

MATHEMATICS
- **Investigate comparisons** in size and weight, and the vocabulary involved: small, smaller, smallest; big, bigger, biggest; light, lighter, lightest, etc.

Who is bigger than Little Billy Goat Gruff ?

A troll needs —
1. A round head
2. A round body.
3. Two long arms.
4. Two short legs.
5. Two horns.
6. Lots of spikes.
7. Hair or fur.
8. A cross face.

My Troll is called Carlie

- Order the goats in terms of size. Match the goats to bells, horns, buckets, etc., in terms of size.
- Investigate problems. For example, what would have happened if the goats had been heavier? Would the bridge have been strong enough?
- Learn ordinal numbers, for example, first, second, third, etc.
- Investigate Number 3. Count in threes. Sort items into threes. Make patterns with three objects. How many different ways can three unifix cubes be fitted together? How many colour combinations can be used?
- Addition and subtraction. Investigate 'stories about 3' as each Billy Goat Gruff crosses the river . For example, $1+2=3$, $2+1=3$, $3+0=3$, $3-1=2$, $3-2=1$, $3-3=0$.
- **Sort into sets things that float**, and things that sink. Record this with set rings and in written form (see Science).

These things float

These things sink

SCIENCE

- Explore what goats as living creatures need to survive, for example, fresh grass and water. Compare with other animals and with ourselves.
- Investigate which materials float or sink. Predict and test outcomes, and record. Sort into sets.
- Which materials could the Billy Goats use to try to cross the river? Which ones would not be suitable, and why?
- Investigate displacement of water. Mark water level with an elastic band round the jar. Put in a 'troll'. What has happened to the water level?
- Discuss safety issues with regard to water.

HUMANITIES - History and Geography

- **Make a map of the route** the Billy Goats took across the bridge to the other side of the river, with the teacher initially drawing the map. Raise questions such as: How can we show the river? What shall we draw for the bridge? How do we know which way the goats went? How can we show this (for example, arrows)? Devise a simple key.

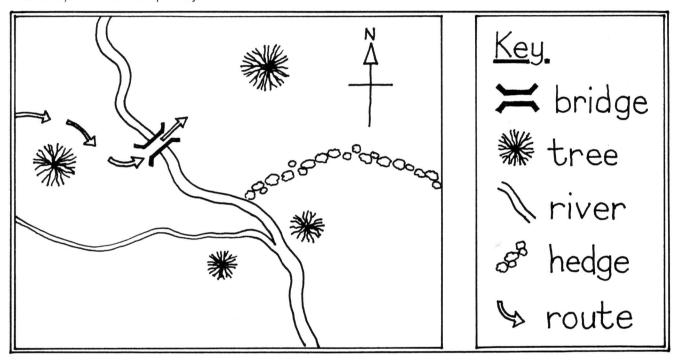

- The follow-up activities can be appropriately differentiated. For example, some children could make up their own map with symbols and a simple key. Others can put the symbols that the teacher has introduced onto a prepared worksheet, and label this.
- Make a large baseboard map to use on the floor. The children could build a bridge using construction toys, and move toy goats along a route over the bridge. They could find the longest and the shortest routes.

DESIGN AND TECHNOLOGY

- Draw up the specifications for a Troll with the class. What is essential? Design a Troll to meet these specifications.
- Make a 2-dimensional drawing.
- Use a range of materials to make a 3-dimensional model (see photograph on page 39).
- Explore different ways of joining materials.
- Use a variety of construction toys to build bridges across the river. Which materials and which designs make the strongest bridges? Predict and use a fair test to find out, and record if appropriate.
- Build bridges out of a variety of found materials. Predict and use a fair test to find the strongest.

- Find out about the design of real bridges. Look at photographs of them. Why are they built to a particular design? What are they made of?
- **Investigate alternative ways of crossing the river.** Record ideas in pictorial or written form. Make models out of wood, card and other materials (see photograph). Evaluate the ideas.
- Record in pictorial and written form the materials used and the way the models were put together.

ART AND CRAFT
- Make a class picture of the Troll under the bridge and the Billy Goats Gruff, using collage materials (see photograph on page 37). Label with positional words. Investigate different textures and patterns.
- Paint or draw posters warning others about the Troll.
- Make a Troll mask which will frighten others!
- Make observational drawings of bridges built and models made.
- Paint or draw pictures to illustrate aspects of the story. Illustrate a class book.
- Look at illustrations in books about Trolls and other fictional 'monsters'. What do the pictures tell us?

P.E. AND MOVEMENT
- Link P.E. and movement activities with work on prepositions. Use small apparatus, for example, work with hoops. Stand in, outside, next to, in front of, and behind the hoop. Jump in, out, over, across and through the hoop. Use large apparatus. Move under, over, above, across, up, down, etc. Work in pairs. Stand next to, behind, in front of, etc.
- Investigate alternative ways for the goats to cross the river through movement and drama, for example, using stepping stones, making a raft, felling a tree, etc.

MUSIC
- Take rhythmic phrases and refrains in the story and clap these. Extend through use of percussion instruments. Which instruments would be suitable for which characters?
- Investigate other rhythms using words or phrases as a basis, for example, children's names, lines of poetry, etc. Guess the child's name from the rhythm.

THE UGLY DUCKLING

(Story source - Hans Christian Andersen, Denmark)

Resumé of Story

Mother duck is sitting on her eggs in the nest to keep them warm. One by one the chicks hatch from the eggs until only the biggest one is left. From that egg hatches a duckling which is very different from the rest. He is not yellow, small and fluffy, but grey and brown, large and ugly.

The Ugly Duckling is laughed at by his family and the other animals in the farmyard because he is different. At last he is so unhappy that he leaves them and goes out into the wider world. He finds a lake where the wild ducks live and he stays there, feeling very lonely, until winter comes. It is so cold that he becomes frozen in the ice and is saved by a farmer who takes him home.

The Ugly Duckling is so frightened in the farmhouse that he knocks over the milk, gets into the butter and flour and makes a mess, before being chased out by the farmer's wife and children.

Eventually, Spring comes and the Ugly Duckling sees three beautiful swans swimming on the lake. Suddenly he sees there are four reflections of swans in the water, and realises that he has changed into a beautiful swan. He has found new friends at last.

Telling the Story

• Emphasise the attitudes and feelings of the characters in the story by use of voice and gesture.
• Involve the children in participating in these feelings through questions and suggestions. For example, 'How did the Ugly Duckling feel when everyone laughed at him? Show me how he felt by using your face and your body.'
• Encourage the children to predict what will happen next, and how the Ugly Duckling will feel.
• Read different versions of the story. Compare the plot and the differences in illustrations and vocabulary. Seek children's own views on the books. Which illustrations did they like best? Which author re-told the story best?

Theme of Story (PSE/RE issues)
• Respecting the differences between one another.
• Not judging by outward appearances.
• The importance of getting to know other people well. Relate this to the children's own experiences.

Assembly Ideas
• Tell the story - teacher or individual children. Use a small group of children to act the story and provide mime or dialogue. Simple masks and wings provide suitable dramatic aids.
• Alternatively, children can mime to 'The Ugly Duckling' song, either sung by other members of the class or played on tape (or the song can be sung afterwards).
• Show paintings and collages to reinforce the sequence of the story and the contrasts within it, for example, happy/sad, winter/summer, gosling/swan, etc.
• What makes us feel happy or sad?
• How do we feel if others laugh at us in an unkind way, or won't be friends? What is it like to be alone?

Further themes
• Links with new life and new beginnings as symbolised by the egg.
• Links with Easter celebrations.
• Links with the concept of change. How can we change for the better?

ENGLISH
Speaking and Listening
• Discuss differences between people, and their similarities, and emphasise descriptive words.
• Use a 'circle time' approach to explore things that make us feel happy or sad.
  For example, 'I feel happy/sad/lonely when...'

Reading and Writing

• Re-tell the story in pictorial and/or written form, depending on ability. **Provide a format to aid sequencing.**

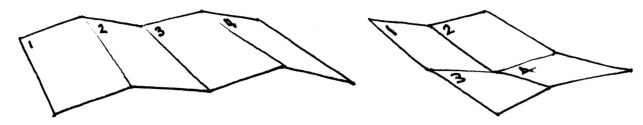

• Re-tell an episode from the story using speech bubbles to show what each character might have said or thought.
• Use a wordbank or chart to support emergent writing containing words relevant to the story. Use a class wordbank, chart or table-top cards to help children with frequently used key words.
• Use reference books to find out about birds and their life cycles. Record what you have found out - as a contribution to a class book or display.
• Use reference books to find out about other creatures who lay eggs.
• Collect other versions of the story. Compare these.
• Collect poems, rhymes and songs about birds and eggs. Learn some as a class and say them together. Others can be read out to the class by individual children.
• Investigate and list words that end in 'ing' as in 'duckling'. Learning this spelling pattern.

• Write and draw about the changes that occur in ourselves as we grow. Make comparisons between different stages.

MATHEMATICS

- Investigate reflections and symmetry.
- **Introduce addition and subtraction** activities to 10, using number of eggs in a nest. For example, '6 eggs in a nest, 2 hatch out. How many are left?'

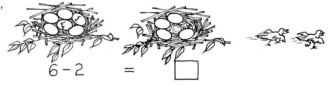

- Problem-solving activities. For example, **'How many different ways can you put four eggs in the egg box?'**

- Time activities. For example: time the cooking of a boiled egg with different measures - egg-timer, clock, kitchen timer. Emphasise vocabulary of time - seconds, minutes, hours.

SCIENCE
Change - Life Cycles

- Find out about different birds, their life cycles, their food, habitat and nests. Use books and videos.
- Investigate in detail one common species of bird.
- Find out about the development of the embryo inside a hen's egg. Use appropriate reference material. How long does it take? Which parts develop first?
- Investigate the life cycles of other creatures and how they change. What other creatures lay eggs? (See photograph above.)
- Look in depth at how babies grow into toddlers, then into children and finally into adults. How have we changed since we were babies? What can we do now that we could not do before? (See photograph on facing page.) Make a display of photographs of children at different ages to show development.

HUMANITIES - History and Geography
- Look at the concepts of past, present, future, before and after, in relation to life cycles of birds and other creatures, including ourselves.
- Make a time-line of our own development. How have we changed? What could we not do in the past that we can do now? What else might we be able to do in the future?
- Invite a mother into school to talk about her baby's development and care.
- Investigate family trees, with the help of parents. Learn vocabulary related to families, for example, cousin, aunty, uncle, nephew, niece, etc.
- Discuss what job you would like to do when you are grown up. Find out about the job.
- Discuss how we respond to seasonal changes in climate, particularly in relation to clothes, food and leisure activities.

DESIGN AND TECHNOLOGY

Boil the water.   Time the cooking.   Put in the egg cup.

- **Cook an egg** in different ways (fried, boiled, poached, scrambled, etc.). What is needed to cook the egg? For example, water, a saucepan and a heat source are needed to boil an egg. What is needed in order to eat it? How effective is this method of cooking, and how suitable are the implements used? Record the cooking methods used in writing and drawing, as a class or individual activity.

ART AND CRAFT
- Make a class picture of the Ugly Duckling and of the swan he turned into, using many different types of paper (for example, tissue, foil, crêpe, card, sugar paper, cartridge paper). Curl thick paper for the birds' feathers around pencils, and glue on (see photographs - page 42 and 43).
- Look at patterns and textures on birds and other creatures that lay eggs.
- Make a creature that hatches from an egg, using own choice of media, either individually or with a partner (see photograph on page 45).
- Paint pictures of different seasons to illustrate the changes that occur. Use cooler colours for colder weather and warmer colours for warm weather.

P.E. AND MOVEMENT
- Move like a baby, a toddler, a child and a grown-up. Why do we move in different ways at different stages of our development?
- Build the idea of change into movement and P.E. - by changing direction, changing level, changing speed, etc.
- Practise balancing skills, like a bird on a perch.

MUSIC
- Learn songs about ducks and birds, including 'There once was an ugly duckling'. Devise actions to accompany songs with the children.
- Investigate contrasts in music in terms of tempo, rhythm, pitch - using percussion instruments, hands and voices.
- Listen and move to music which illustrates the different seasons, for example, Vivaldi's 'The Four Seasons'.

THE TOWN MOUSE AND THE COUNTRY MOUSE

(Story Source - based on an Aesop fable)

Resumé of Story

The Town Mouse comes to visit the Country Mouse but does not enjoy his stay. Everything is different: he finds Country Mouse's home uncomfortable; he does not like searching for and eating nuts and berries; he is frightened by a horse and nearly caught by an owl.

He returns to the town and invites Country Mouse to go with him. Country Mouse in his turn does not like the town: he does not like living in a human's house; he does not like the rich food stolen from the people; he is nearly run over by a car and eaten by a cat. He returns home to the country with which he is familiar, and where he is happy.

Telling the Story

Tell the story in two parts, one from the Country Mouse's point of view, and one from the Town Mouse's point of view. Emphasise the contrasts between their lifestyles and their characters. Use gesture and voice contrasts to emphasise this.

Re-tell the story with the children's help from the point of view of the host rather than the visitor in each case.

Theme of Story (PSE/RE issues)
• The need to respect the lifestyles and customs of others.

Assembly
• Tell or act the story, using children as the two mice to mime or to voice their likes and dislikes.
• Establish one area for the town, another for the country. Children could show paintings and other artwork to the audience to illustrate the differences in home, habitat, food and the possible dangers (see photograph on page 47).
• Explore the contrasts between the town and the country. Involve the audience.
• Explore the idea of contrasts in terms of likes and dislikes, feelings and emotions.
• Celebrate the differences between individuals and between cultures and countries.
• Issues to consider: Why did each mouse find it difficult to understand what the other mouse liked? Why did each mouse think he was right? Do we find it difficult to see things from somebody else's point of view? What do we find interesting about other people, other cultures and other countries?

Speaking and Listening
• With the children's help, set up two areas within the classroom, one as the Country Mouse's home, and one as the Town Mouse's home. Encourage children to dramatise the story by playing host or visitor in each home, using appropriate vocabulary. Encourage them to prepare for a journey to and from the other home.
• Provide opportunities for the children to pretend to be one of the mice and to describe their home, food, enemies and environment and their way of life to adults and peers.
• Discuss the contrasts in lifestyles between the two mice, looking at comparative vocabulary and phrases.
• **Draw up a list of words and their opposites.**

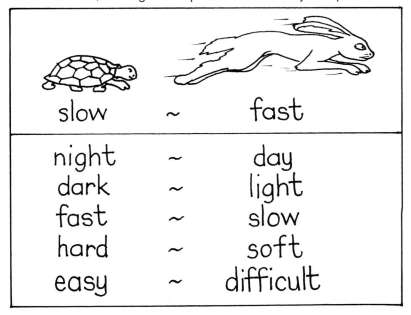

slow	~	fast
night	~	day
dark	~	light
fast	~	slow
hard	~	soft
easy	~	difficult

Further Discussion Points
• Discuss different homes and environments for people, starting with the children's own experience.
• Discuss the differences between the town and the country for people as well as for animals.

ENGLISH
Reading and Writing
• Re-tell the story from one mouse's point of view, using pictures and words.
• Write or draw (depending on ability) - outlining the lifestyle of one of the mice (home, food, enemies, habitat, etc.).

- Write a poem about one of the mice, beginning 'I am a town/country mouse.....', or write a class poem.
- Make two lists to compare the different lifestyles of the two mice (see photograph page 47).
- Write invitations from one mouse to another, using correct format, and make up an address for each (see photograph page 50).
- **Describe the journey from one mouse's home to another, in words and pictures.**

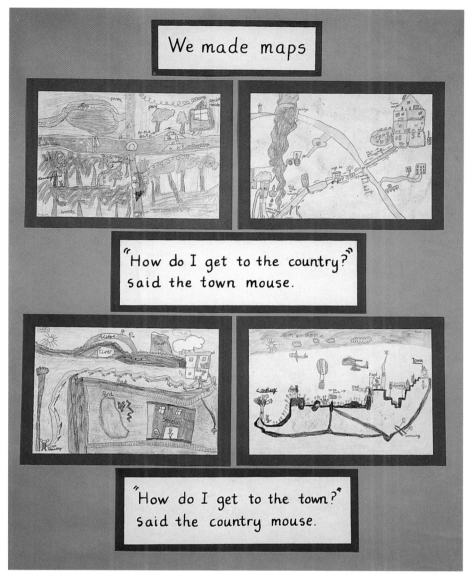

- Collect and read poems and stories about mice.
- Collect and read non-fiction books about different sorts of mice who live in different habitats.
- Explore books about homes for animals and people.

MATHEMATICS
- Collect data about the type of homes the children live in. Make a bar graph to show this. Examine and discuss data with the children.
- Investigate time. How long did it take each mouse to get to the other's house? How long did they spend there? Use time vocabulary (a long/short time, later, earlier, yesterday, tomorrow, hours, minutes, days and weeks).
- Discuss house numbers and, in particular, odd and even numbers. What are the numbers of the children's houses, flats, etc?

HUMANITIES - History and Geography
- Make individual maps and a class map to show the journeys of the mice to one another's homes. Use simple co-ordinates to find the positions of various points on the map. Encourage children to describe the journey their mouse has taken (see photograph above).

- Look at occupations in the town and in the country, and compare them.
- Encourage children to describe journeys they have made.
- Compare homes of today with past homes. Collect domestic items of different periods and arrange them on a time-line, for example, washing and cleaning artefacts.

DESIGN AND TECHNOLOGY
- Design and make a vehicle so that the journey is easier for the mice.
- Food technology. Make up a menu for each mouse. Design tableware and settings for the town and country.
- Make a town house and country house out of waste materials. Make a baseboard map for them with the route between drawn out. Make Plasticine mice to travel between the houses.
- **Design notepaper and envelope to send invitations from one mouse to another (see photograph).**

ART AND CRAFT
- Make a class picture, using paint and wax resist, showing the contrasts between lifestyles of the mice.
- Make town and country rubbings using crayons and paper: for example, bark, leaves, bricks, paving stones, etc. Sort and mount these in the classroom.
- Look at the work of famous artists to compare town and country, for example: Lowry - town, and Constable - country.

P.E. AND MOVEMENT
- Use P.E. time to investigate given routes, and to make up own routes. Emphasise vocabulary, for example, straight, crooked, left, right, forwards, backwards, turning.
- How do mice move? Move in that way, for example, scurrying and freezing on the word 'cat'. Move like other wild animals. Contrasts qualities of movement.
- Make a sequence of movements for a mouse, for example, sitting up, scurrying, freezing, twitching whiskers, etc.

MUSIC
- Interpret country and town sounds with instruments, to make a sound story of the route between the houses.
- Make mouse-like sounds using instruments. On a signal (for example, cymbals), stop playing and keep silent (as cat has arrived).
- Find songs and rhymes about mice and cats.

THE RABBIT WHO STOLE THE FIRE

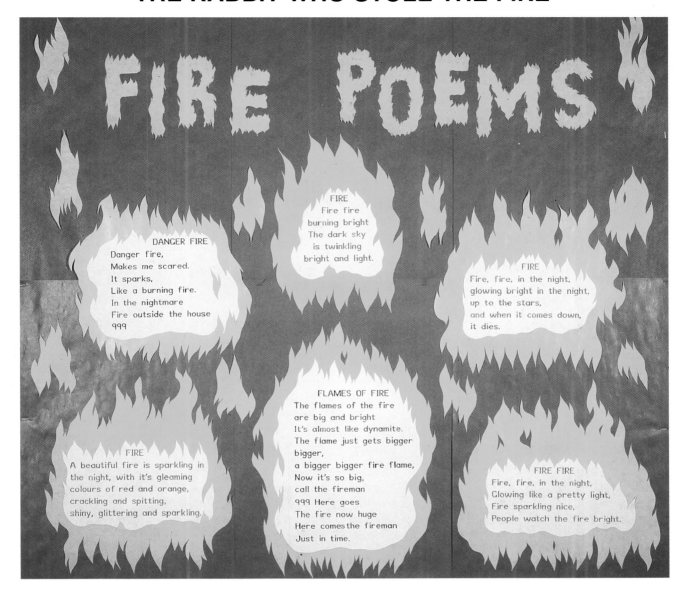

FIRE POEMS

DANGER FIRE
Danger fire,
Makes me scared.
It sparks,
Like a burning fire.
In the nightmare
Fire outside the house
999

FIRE
Fire fire
burning bright
The dark sky
is twinkling
bright and light.

FIRE
Fire, fire, in the night,
glowing bright in the night,
up to the stars,
and when it comes down,
it dies.

FIRE
A beautiful fire is sparkling in
the night, with it's gleaming
colours of red and orange,
crackling and spitting,
shiny, glittering and sparkling.

FLAMES OF FIRE
The flames of the fire
are big and bright
It's almost like dynamite.
The flame just gets bigger
bigger,
a bigger bigger fire flame,
Now it's so big,
call the fireman
999 Here goes
The fire now huge
Here comes the fireman
Just in time.

FIRE FIRE
Fire, fire, in the night,
Glowing like a pretty light,
Fire sparkling nice,
People watch the fire bright.

(Story Source - Native American story)

Story Resumé

It is winter. The animals are cold and they need fire. The Sky People have fire but they will not share it with the animals. Rabbit, the chief mischief-maker, thinks of a daring plan. He makes a head-dress of feathers dipped in pine resin, then he goes to visit the Sky People.

The Sky People are suspicious of Rabbit at first, but his cunning words make them forget their suspicions and he joins them in a dance around the fire. Suddenly, Rabbit is off, with the head-dress of feathers and resin alight.

The Sky People give chase, but with the help of his friends (squirrel, crow, raccoon, turkey and deer), Rabbit's plan has worked, he has stolen the fire, and the animals are no longer cold.

Telling the Story

• Sit in a circle to listen to the story as though you are around a fire, setting the story in context.
• Choose children to mime aspects of the story: animals shivering, then dancing around the fire, animals warmed by the fire, etc.
• Use percussion instruments in telling the story - children can join in, for example, using drums for dancing.

Theme of Story (PSE/RE issues)

• Sharing with others. Who was right and who was wrong in the story? (Is it possible to say?)

The animals did not have fire. They were cold.

The sky people would not give them fire.

How rabbit stole the fire

Assembly Ideas
- Tell the story and act using simple masks for animals, and feather head-dresses for Rabbit and the Sky People.
- Issues to consider: Were the Sky People right or wrong in not sharing the fire? Was Rabbit wrong in stealing it? Could there have been a better way?

Further Discussion Points
- Fire. Why do we need fire? Can it be harmful or helpful? Which materials burn quickly and which burn more slowly? Talk about fire safety.
- What are the benefits of sharing?

READING AND WRITING
Writing for different purposes
- Brainstorm words to describe fire. Write poems about fire, using word list as an aid. Make a class poetry book about fire. Make a display of the poems for children to share. Read the poems to younger children.
- Re-tell story in written and pictorial form, sequencing events correctly. A concertina book is a good format for this. Re-tell the 'chase' section of the story, with the animals who helped Rabbit in the right order. Record how the animals changed as a result of helping Rabbit. For example, the squirrel's long straight tail curved up over his back.
- Draw up a Fire Safety Code. Make a poster to inform others (see Art and Craft).
- Read some short extracts from the poem 'Hiawatha', by H.W. Longfellow.

MATHEMATICS
- Tables. Two times: How many ears have Rabbit's friends altogether? Four times: How many paws?
- Make head-dresses with feathers - measuring head sizes (using non-standard and standard measurements).

The animals took the fire and hid it.

The animals had fire to keep them warm.

- Sequence Rabbit's helpers correctly. Use ordinal numbers - first, second, third.
- **Work on number bonds to 10 or 20**, using 'feather' sums.

SCIENCE
- Discuss properties of fire. How can it help us? How can it harm us? How can we use it?
- What does a fire need in order to burn (ignition, oxygen, material)?
- What should we do if there is a fire? Draw up a Fire Safety Code. Find out about the fire precautions in the school, and the fire drill. Find out about First Aid.
- Discuss the dangers of playing with matches or fireworks. Make posters telling others.
- Discuss which materials burn quickly and which burn more slowly. How do we use these materials in everyday life (buildings, etc.)? What are these materials like? What are the similarities and differences between them? Can we group them in other ways? What do we make from these materials?
- How did the Native Americans use the materials in their environment? What did they make? Which materials did they not have?

DESIGN AND TECHNOLOGY
- Discuss how effective Rabbit's feather and resin head-dress was. What else could Rabbit have used? How would Rabbit have constructed it?

- Make feather headbands or head-dresses. Plan, make and evaluate. Test that they fit - perhaps run with them on! Compare designs.

HUMANITIES - History and Geography
- Discuss how Native Americans lived in harmony with their environment. (Choose a particular region to illustrate this - for example, Plains Native Americans.) How did they use the materials around them to make the things they needed to live?
- Discuss precautions taken against fire in the town and in the country.
- Investigate historical events: Guy Fawkes and the Gunpowder Plot; the Great Fire of London.
- Discuss problems that fire can cause in other countries, for example, bushfires in Australia, and discuss the reasons why they occur.
- Discuss the job of the firefighters. What clothing and equipment do they need? What training do they need?
- Make a map to illustrate where Rabbit went.

ART AND CRAFT
- Make a class picture to illustrate the story, and to put the events in sequence. Make a border of animals. Use pastels and crayons. (See photographs on page 52 and 53.)
- Make pictures of fire using different media: crêpe and tissue paper, thick paint and spatulas, crayons and pastels, charcoal.
- Make a feather collage.
- Make masks of the animals for drama.
- **Make a poster giving information about fire and its uses** (see photograph).

P.E., DRAMA, MOVEMENT
- Move like animals in the story. Hop like rabbits, run like deer, etc.
- Make up your own fire dance to music.
- Move like flames in a fire. Move like the smoke.

MUSIC
- Use percussion instruments to illustrate the story musically. What instruments would you use for Rabbit and for the other animals? What instruments would you use for the dance?
- Learn songs and rhymes on the theme of fire - for example, 'London's burning'.

TIDDALIK

'I am so thirsty I could drink a lake,' said Tiddalik, and that is what he did

(Story source - an Australian Aboriginal Dreamtime story)

Resumé of Story

In the Dreamtime, long ago, lived a large frog called Tiddalik. Tiddalik was thirsty; so thirsty that he drank all the water until the land was dry. The animals met to decide what to do. They decided they must make Tiddalik laugh. How could they do this? Not one animal succeeded until Platypus, emerging from her burrow to see what all the fuss was about, made Tiddalik laugh because of her strange appearance. Out came the water from Tiddalik's great mouth, and soon there was enough water in the lakes and rivers for everyone. Since then, there have only been small frogs in Australia. They survive by drinking and storing water in their bodies in the drought, but they only take their fair share.

Telling the Story

- Set the story in context. Describe the Australian outback, and droughts, and explain how precious water is - especially during a drought. Talk about the use of stories by the Aborigines to explain what happens in the world around them.
- Encourage the children to join in with parts of the story, and to suggest what Tiddalik, Platypus and each animal might have said.
- Dramatise the story, using simple masks made by the children.
- Use musical instruments to provide music for the story, to describe events such as Tiddalik laughing and letting the water rush out of his mouth.

Theme of Story (PSE/RE issues)

- The importance of sharing.

Assembly Ideas
- Tell the story and act using simple masks for the animals and birds.
- Discuss the issues. Was it right for Tiddalik to drink all the water? What should he have done? The animals co-operated to find a solution. They decided to make Tiddalik laugh. How else could they make him open his mouth? Are some ways kinder than others? How can we share with other people? In what ways can we share in school?
- What makes us laugh? Why might we want to make someone else laugh?

ENGLISH
Speaking and Listening
- Children re-tell the story individually or as a group, providing their own words for each character to say.
- Children re-tell the story but substitute their own idea of how to make Tiddalik open his mouth.
- Discuss the story. What is Tiddalik like as a character? How could he change?
- What would it be like to be thirsty in a drought? How would you feel? What would you do?
- Discuss Australian words and their meanings, for example, billabong, tucker, etc.

Discussion Points
- Why do all creatures need water to live? What can water do? How do we use it?
- What do we know about Australia? What do we know about the animals there? Who are the Aborigines? How do they live?
- What do we know about the frogs that live in our country?
- What makes us laugh? How can we make other people laugh? Is laughter always kind?

Reading and Writing
- **Re-tell the story in written and pictorial form** using speech bubbles to show what Tiddalik and the animals are saying.

- Write and illustrate a joke which would make somebody else laugh. Make a class joke book.
- Make a list of the ways in which we can make someone laugh.
- Write and draw about an incident that made us laugh. Make a class book to share with others.
- Write a list of words to describe what water can do. Make posters to illustrate each of these words, with writing and pictures which conveys the meanings of the words. Make a display (see photograph on page 58).
- Using reference books, write about and illustrate the life cycle of the frog or toad. This could be done in pairs. Make a class display with tadpoles, books about frogs and pond life (see photograph page 59).

MATHEMATICS
- Conservation of capacity. Compare different shaped containers of the same capacity. Introduce formal measures - litre and half litres.
- Measurement of flow. Estimate and time how long it takes to empty containers with wide or narrow necks holding the same quantity.
- Reflections (in water). Use mirrors to show reflections and symmetry.
- Fold a piece of paper in half lengthways and draw a simple picture showing a reflection in water.
- Make symmetrical patterns, similar to Aboriginal patterns, using lines, dots and shapes (see photograph above).
- Make symmetrical patterns with mosaics.
- Colour in mosaic worksheet to make a symmetrical pattern.

SCIENCE
- Discuss properties of water, and carry out experiments to illustrate these. What can water do? How can it change (melt, freeze)? How can it change other things (extinguish fires, dissolve solids, suspend)? Record experiments.

- Investigate uses of water, for example, drinking, washing, travelling, cleaning, extinguishing fire, cooking, heating.
- Where do we find water (lakes, ponds, rivers, seas, oceans, rain, water vapour, snow, ice, mist, liquids)?

- **Make a picture of the water cycle.** Label the diagram.

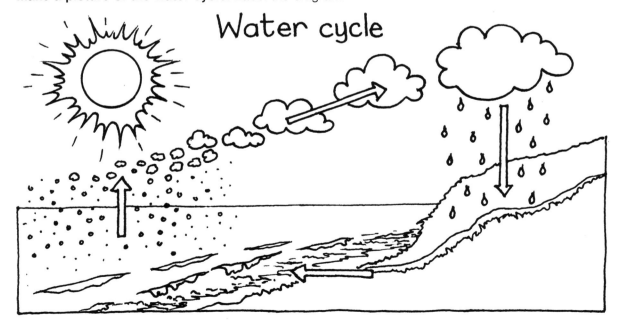

- How is water purified? How does the water get to our homes? How is the dirty water taken away? How is water conserved?

The young frogs come out of the water.

The frogs catch insects and grow.

The frogs mate and lay frogspawn.

The life cycle of the frog.

The tadpoles hatch out

The tadpoles grow back and front legs.

The tadpoles develop inside the jelly.

- **The life cycle of the frog.** Find out how the tadpole changes to become a frog, and then lives in a different environment. How do creatures adapt to live in a particular environment. What do we need to provide for tadpoles to live in a tank? Observe the tadpoles changing to frogs. Log the changes, and record in writing and pictures (see photograph).
- Floating and sinking. Which materials float? Which sink? Hypothesise, test, and record findings.

DESIGN AND TECHNOLOGY
- Design a water run with lengths of piping and hose.
- Make animal masks for drama (see photograph on page 60).
- Design a boat that will float (using waste materials).

HUMANITIES - History and Geography
- Locate Australia on a map or globe. How can we get there?
- Look at different climates in the world. Compare the Australian outback climate with ours.
- Find out about Australia, using reference material (books, artefacts, pictures, videos and music). Make a display of the material to inform other classes or visitors to the school. Write and illustrate the facts. Label the items in the display. (See photograph on page 57.)
- Compare own locality with a locality in Australia, for example, the outback, or the rainforests.
- Look for similarities and differences in climate, geology, vegetation, wildlife, settlement and land use, population, transport and language.
- Find out about the Aborigines and their culture and beliefs.

ART AND CRAFT

- Make a class picture illustrating a scene from the story of Tiddalik. (Chalk and pastels give a hazy, dry and hot effect.)
- Make a frieze illustrating main events from the story, in sequence.
- Make paper collage pictures of the life cycle of the frog to form a display (see photograph page 59).
- Use reference books and pictures, making detailed drawings of Australian animals and birds.
- Investigate Aboriginal art, using books, posters and artefacts. Look at the symbolism and the techniques, colours and materials used.
- Make Aboriginal pictures using pencil ends as painting sticks to make symbols and shapes which have a meaning. Name the pictures.
- Look at famous paintings of water, for example, Monet's 'Waterlilies', Seurat's pointillist paintings of rivers, and notice how the weather and the time of day are indicated by the colours and tones used. Make your own versions using different media, for example, pastels, chalks, crayons, paint.

P.E., MOVEMENT

- Respond in movement to words that describe what water can do - trickling, dripping, flooding, pouring, rushing.
- Move like Australian animals and birds - jumping like a kangaroo, climbing like a koala, etc. Play a guessing game. Which animal am I?

MUSIC

- Use musical instruments to illustrate the things that water can do, for example, dripping, pouring, trickling, crashing.
- Learn songs and rhymes about water, including sea-shanties and boating songs.
- Learn Australian songs, for example, 'Waltzing Matilda'.
- Listen to Aboriginal music and learn about the didgeridoo.

ANANSI AND MISS LOUISE

(Story source - An Afro-Caribbean story - other Anansi stories could be substituted for this book)

Resumé of Story

(There are many Anansi stories in the Afro-Caribbean culture. Anansi is a trickster who usually gets the better of those around him. Sometimes he is portrayed as a man, sometimes as a spider.)

In this story, Anansi wants to marry the beautiful but sad Miss Louise, but so does Mr Dry-Bones, the magician. She will marry whoever makes her laugh. Mr Dry-Bones tries all sorts of magic and clever tricks, but Miss Louise does not laugh. Meanwhile, Anansi, who wants to look his best, asks his friends for help. Tiger lends him his best striped suit, crocodile lends him his shoes, parrot gives him a feather, monkey gives him a tie, and dog gives him a hunting hat.

When Anansi arrives at Miss Louise's house he looks so strange in his borrowed clothes that do not fit him that she cannot help laughing. So Anansi wins and marries Miss Louise.

Telling the Story

- Dramatise the story by using mime and body language as well as different voices, to emphasise the personality of each character.
- Use percussion instruments or animal sounds to signal the involvement of a particular character (for example, hollow coconuts for Mr. Dry-Bones), in order to build suspense in the story.
- Use a tape of Caribbean music to set the scene. Involve the children in these sound signals.
- Encourage the children to re-tell and to act out the story themselves.

Theme of Story (PSE/RE issues)

- The importance of help from friends.
- It is not always the most clever person who achieves the most.

Assembly Ideas

- Tell the story and act, using hats for the main characters (top-hat for Mr Dry-Bones, hat with feather for Anansi, scarf for Miss Louise, and clothes for Anansi, given by the animals).
- Accompany with percussion instruments.
- Issues to consider: Who are our friends? Why do we need friends? What are our friends like? Are we good friends to other people?

ENGLISH
Speaking and Listening

- Children re-tell the story as a group, sequencing events correctly and adding their own mimes and sound effects. They could present the story to younger children.
- Teacher writes out the story in a play format, with a script for each character with each part underlined or high-lighted. Children act out the play in small groups and present to one another. Children could be included in drawing up this script and in deciding what each character should say.
- Discuss the story. What do you think each character is like? Who would you like to be friends with? Who would you feel comfortable with?

Further Discussion Points

- Discuss the contrasts between the locality in which we live, and that of the Caribbean. Look at differences in climate, housing, food, music, occupations, lifestyle, language, clothes.
- **Friends. Who are our friends?** Why do we need friends? What are our friends like? Are we good friends to other people?

Reading and Writing

- Re-tell the story in written and/or pictorial form.
- Find and read other stories about Anansi.
- Collect stories and poems from the Caribbean. Read aloud and look at differences in the use of English.
- Collect information and non-fiction books about life in the Caribbean. Make a resource centre.

MATHEMATICS
- Anansi's borrowed clothes looked funny on him because they did not fit. How do we ensure our clothes and shoes fit? Look at shoe sizes, clothes sizes. Consider informal measures (for example, hand spans) and formal measures.
- Draw a 'Treasure Island' map (see photograph on page 64) using co-ordinates to plot the position of different features on the island. Read one another's maps. Guess where the treasure is hidden.
- Plan a route across the island to collect the treasure and bring it back to the ship. Describe the route in terms of features encountered and corresponding co-ordinate positions.
- Consider money values. What coins and notes do we have in our currency? What is their value in relation to one another? Make up your own currency - naming coins and notes and allocating values to them.

SCIENCE
- Compare the environment in one of the Caribbean islands with our own environment. What are the differences in climate, vegetation, soil, etc. What plants grow and what animals, fish and birds live there? How do people use their environment in the Caribbean, and in our own local area?
- Look at materials used. What materials do people use for housing and for clothing in the Caribbean and in our own locality? Why are there differences or similarities?
- Collect Caribbean recipes. Try some of these by cooking and preparing food in small groups. Taste the dishes and describe the taste to others. (Note: First check for any allergies to food amongst the children.)

DESIGN AND TECHNOLOGY
- Make a 3-dimensional map of a treasure island from a 2-dimensional plan - using boxes and papier mâché on a base of hardboard or similar. Paint and varnish to finish.

- Make percussion instruments to accompany Caribbean music and rhymes. Shakers can be made out of two plastic food containers such as yogurt pots, filled with rice, beans, pasta, etc. (to give different sounds) and glued together and painted. Rhythm sticks can be made from pieces of dowelling. Halved coconut shells can be used. Drums can be made out of metal biscuit tins, etc. (See photograph page 2.)

HUMANITIES - History and Geography

- Compare your own locality with that of the Caribbean. What are the differences? What are the similarities? Consider climate, food and vegetables, homes, occupations, music, language, people, clothes, etc.
- Make a collection and display of Caribbean food produce and products made from these, both well-known and less well-known, for example, sugar cane, sugar, rum, bananas, pineapples, mangoes, spices (see photograph on page 63). Collect recipes which use these products, both from your home country and from the Caribbean. Choose some dishes to cook and to taste in school.
- Consider the importance of tourism in the Caribbean. Look at holiday brochures. Why is the Caribbean a good place for a holiday? What can it offer? Are there any drawbacks? What would you do on holiday there? Make up your own poster or brochure to attract people to the Caribbean, or to your own local area.
- Consider the history of the Caribbean. Where did the people come from, and who lives there now? Why did they come? What culture did they bring with them? What do you think about slavery? Draw up a time-line. Look at how transport has changed between the Caribbean and other parts of the world.
- **Make up your own imaginary island and draw a map of it.** What symbols will you use to show the geographical features on your island? Devise a key to explain these.

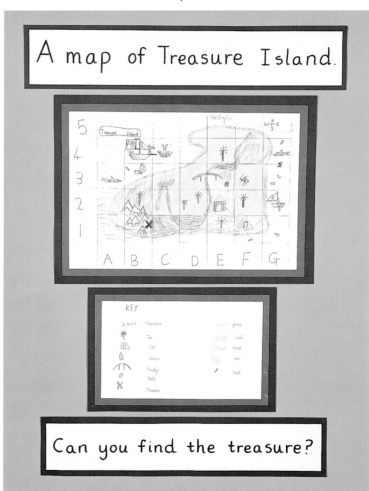

- Look at maps, particularly of islands. What do maps tell us? What symbols do they use for features such as roads, hills, beaches, cliffs, etc? What are the co-ordinates on a map? How do we use them to find things?
- Look at a map of the world. Locate your own country and the Caribbean countries on it. How would you get from your country to go on holiday to the Caribbean?

ART AND CRAFT

- Make a class picture to illustrate an aspect of the story or to emphasise the personalities of the characters. Make a trellis border of folded and cut black paper. Use mixed media of felt-tip pens and paint (see photograph on page 61).

- Plan and make pictures in pairs to illustrate the differences between the Caribbean and your own locality, using own choice of media (see photograph above).
- Make life drawings of Caribbean fruits and vegetables, whole and halved, using crayons and pastels (see photograph on page 63).
- Make posters to advertise a holiday in the Caribbean.

MUSIC
- Listen to Caribbean music, including reggae, steel bands and rap. Discuss the instruments being used and what they are made of. Explore the rhythms of the music, clapping alongside or in echo. Move to the rhythm. Play percussion instruments, making up your own rhythm.
- Make up your own rap song as a class, using your own instruments. Record and evaluate (see photograph on page 2).

P.E./DRAMA/MOVEMENT
- Move like the characters in the story. Can you do tricks like Mr Dry-Bones? How did Anansi move in the clothes which were the wrong size for him?
- Make up your own dance to move to Caribbean rhythms: individually, in pairs, in a group or as a class.
- Use the instruments you have made to accompany songs, stories and rhymes, and also the rap song you have composed.

THE WIZARD PUNCHKIN

(Story source - An Indian tale of the battle between good and evil)

Resumé of Story

Chandra, an Indian prince, sets out one day to find his six elder brothers who had disappeared many years earlier. He journeys to the north to where the Wizard Punchkin lives. On his way he saves a nest of young eagles from a serpent, and the parent eagles give him, as a reward, a magic feather with which he can summon them whenever he needs help.

At last Chandra comes to a stony wasteland where he finds his six brothers amongst many other people and animals, but they have all been turned to stone by the Wizard. He summons the eagle to fly him over the wasteland to the Wizard's palace. There he finds Laili, a princess, who has been imprisoned by the Wizard, until she promises to marry him.

Chandra plans to defeat the Wizard, but cannot succeed because the Wizard keeps his soul outside his body, hidden in a secret place. When the Wizard returns, Laili promises to be his wife if he tells her where his soul is hidden. He does so and Chandra, who is in hiding, secretly summons the eagle to carry him to where the soul is hidden on an island in an ocean, protected by tigers. It is inside an egg, which is underneath a parrot in a cage.

Chandra seizes the cage with the egg inside, and back at the Wizard's palace squeezes the egg until it cracks, and Punchkin dies.

The spell is broken, the stone figures come to life and Chandra marries Laili.

Telling the Story

- Set the scene using Indian music.
- Invite an Indian guest speaker to tell a story from his or her culture.
- Play Indian music.

Theme of Story (PSE/RE issues)

- The triumph of good over evil.
- The importance of helping others.

Assembly Ideas

- Tell the story and mime it using masks and strong body movements, gestures and facial expressions to convey the action of the story and the personalities of the characters.
- Use puppets to mime the story to a smaller group of children with dialogue provided by the puppeteers or their friends.
- Use percussion instruments, where appropriate, to add drama.
- Issues to consider: What did Chandra do that was good? What did Wizard Punchkin do that was bad? How can we help each other? Explore ways of doing this in school.

ENGLISH
Speaking and Listening

- Teacher or child re-tells the story whilst other children mime the actions.
- Using puppets, children in a small group present the play to the rest of the class. The children provide the dialogue.
- Discuss the story. Does it give us a good understanding of what is good and evil? What are the characters like? Do the illustrations in the book help us to know what they are like?

Further discussion points
- Find out about India and aspects of its culture and religions. Look at Indian artefacts.
- Look at patterns and designs in Indian art, including ceramics and textiles.
- Investigate other accounts of the battle between good and evil in stories from other countries and cultures, for example, George and the Dragon.

Reading and Writing
- Re-tell a section of the story in words and pictures, for example, the search for Wizard Punchkin's soul. Recall the details in the correct order. The excerpts are put together to make up the whole story as a class book.
- Write an outline of each character in the story.
- Write about a good alternative hiding place for the Wizard's soul.

MATHEMATICS
- Investigate Indian patterns and designs with reference to shape, symmetry and sequencing, using artefacts, textiles and reference books.
- Make square and oblong tiles with symmetrical designs, using thick card and felt-tip pens.
- Tessellate tiles to make a 'floor'. How many different arrrangements can you make with a given number? Record on squared paper.
- Investigate the properties of 2-dimensional and 3-dimensional shapes. Which shapes will fit together and tessellate. Which will not? Which sort of tessellating patterns do they make?
- Make a series of boxes using nets of different sizes that will fit one inside the other.

- **Use tiles in different ways to explore the concept of multiplication.**

Multiply to make 12

2	X6 =
6	X2 =
3	X4 =
4	X3 =

SCIENCE
- Investigate how Indian foods change during cooking, making chapatis, and heating poppadoms.
- Find out about the wildlife and vegetation in India. Why are some species, for example, tigers, endangered?
- Diwali. Find out about sources and properties of light. Investigate shadows, reflections and colours.

We designed an Indian Sari

HUMANITIES - History and Geography
- Locate India on a world map, in relation to our own country. Discuss the large size of the country and how the regions differ in climate, topography, land use and settlement.
- Investigate aspects of life in India, for example, clothes worn, seasonal variations in climate, houses, agriculture, manufacturing, religions, customs, food and festivals, for example, Diwali.

- **Make a display of Indian artefacts** with reference to books and posters (see photograph).
- Invite a guest speaker to talk about life in India.
- If possible, visit a museum or display about India.
- Investigate parts of the compass. Why do we need these? How do we use a compass? Look at compass points on a map.
- Read and discuss stories about past important events in India.

DESIGN AND TECHNOLOGY
- Make 2-dimensional puppets, with moving arms and legs, of the main characters. Use butterfly clips for the joints. Hold a puppet show.
- Find out how a sari is worn. Demonstrate if possible.
- Design a sari (see photograph on facing page).

ART AND CRAFT
- Use wrapping paper with Indian designs to make a collage picture of the main characters of the story (see photograph on page 67).
- Design a symmetrical tile based on Indian motifs, using felt-tip pens on white card. Laminate.
- Look at the techniques used in India to decorate clothes. Experiment with those techniques in the classroom, for example, batik and mirror embroidery (using silver paper for mirrors).

P.E., MOVEMENT, DRAMA

• Watch a video of dances from India. How do the dancers use their bodies, their arms and legs, their heads and hands? Emphasise that the gestures and movements often convey meaning.
• Listen to Indian music. Select a character from the story and move in a way which conveys that character's personality.
• Explore contrasts in movement.
• Play 'statues' - freezing on a command from Wizard Punchkin.

MUSIC

• Listen to different types of music from India. Investigate the rhythms. Contrast this music with other forms, for example, jazz, classical Western music, etc.
• Find out about the instruments used in India, for example, the sitar. What do they look like? How are they played? What do they sound like?

For details of further Belair publications
please write to
BELAIR PUBLICATIONS LIMITED
P.O. Box 12, TWICKENHAM, TW1 2QL, ENGLAND

For sales and distribution (outside North America and South America)
FOLENS PUBLISHERS
Albert House, Apex Business Centre
Boscombe Road, Dunstable, Bedfordshire, LU5 4RL
England

For sales and distribution in North America and South America
INCENTIVE PUBLICATIONS
3835 Cleghorn Avenue, Nashville, Tn 37215, U.S.A.

For sales and distribution in Australia
EDUCATIONAL SUPPLIES PTY LTD
8 Cross Street, Brookvale, N.S.W. 2100
Australia